D0187796

WITHDRAWN

Alpha Team Guide
© 2016 Alpha International

All rights reserved. No portion of this publication may be reproduced, stored in a retrieval system, or transmitted in any form or by any means—electronic, mechanical, photocopy, recording, scanning, or other—without the prior written consent of the publisher. Where an Alpha publication is offered free of charge, the fee is waived on condition the publication is used to run or promote Alpha and should not be subject to any subsequent fee or charge. This resource may not be modified or used for any commercial purpose without permission in writing from the copyright holder or the expressly authorized agent thereof.

Published in Nashville, Tennessee, by W Publishing Group, an imprint of Thomas Nelson. W Publishing Group and Thomas Nelson are registered trademarks of HarperCollins Christian Publishing, Inc.

All Scripture quotations, unless otherwise indicated, are taken from The Holy Bible, New International Version®, NIV®. Copyright © 1973, 1978, 1984, 2011 by Biblica, Inc.™ Used by permission. All rights reserved worldwide.

Scripture quotations marked GNT taken from the Good News Translation, Second Edition, Copyright 1992 by American Bible Society. Used by Permission.

Scripture quotations marked NLT are taken from are taken from the Holy Bible, New Living Translation, copyright © 1996, 2004, 2007 by Tyndale House Foundation. Used by permission of Tyndale House Publishers, Inc., Carol Stream, Illinois 60188. All rights reserved.

Scripture quotations marked Phillips taken from The New Testament in Modern English, Revised Edition, J. B. Phillips, Translator. © J. B. Phillips 1958, 1960, 1972. Used by permission of Macmillan Publishing Co., Inc., 866 Third Avenue, New York, NY 10022.

ISBN 978-1-938-3-2888-6

First Printing 2016 / Printed in the United States of America

Contents

Section 1	Training	5
Training 1	Small Groups	7
Training 2	Prayer & the Weekend	19
Section 2	Small Group Questions	27
Session 1	Is There More to Life Than This?	32
Session 2	Who Is Jesus?	36
Session 3	Why Did Jesus Die?	38
Session 4	How Can I Have Faith?	40
Session 5	Why and How Do I Pray?	42
Session 6	Why and How Should I Read the Bible?	44
Session 7	How Does God Guide Us?	46
Session 8	Who Is the Holy Spirit?	48
Session 9	What Does the Holy Spirit Do?	50
Session 10	How Can I Be Filled with the Holy Spirit?	52
Session 11	How Can I Make the Most of the Rest of My Life?	54
Session 12	How Can I Resist Evil?	56
Session 13	Why and How Should I Tell Others?	58
Session 14	Does God Heal Today?	60
Session 15	What About the Church?	62
Section 3	Alpha Basics	65

Section 1
Training

Training 1
Small Groups

The aim of this session is to give you all the tools you will need to host or help in an Alpha small group.

The overall purpose of the small group, along with Alpha as a whole, is to help to bring people into a relationship with Jesus Christ by sharing the good news of the gospel (1 Thessalonians 2:2,4,8).

"Alpha is friends bringing friends."

Nicky Gumbel

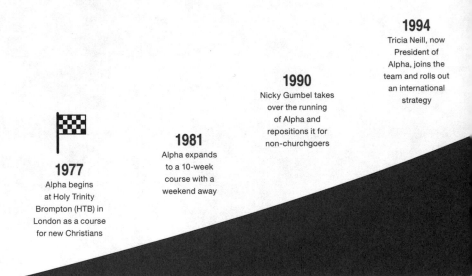

1994
Tricia Neill, now President of Alpha, joins the team and rolls out an international strategy

1990
Nicky Gumbel takes over the running of Alpha and repositions it for non-churchgoers

1981
Alpha expands to a 10-week course with a weekend away

1977
Alpha begins at Holy Trinity Brompton (HTB) in London as a course for new Christians

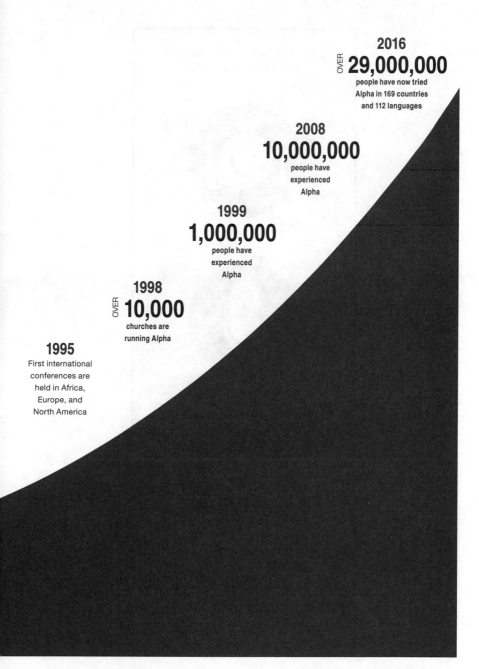

2016
OVER **29,000,000**
people have now tried
Alpha in 169 countries
and 112 languages

2008
10,000,000
people have
experienced
Alpha

1999
1,000,000
people have
experienced
Alpha

1998
OVER **10,000**
churches are
running Alpha

1995
First international
conferences are
held in Africa,
Europe, and
North America

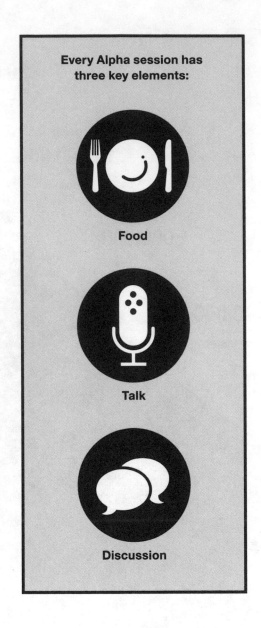

Every Alpha session has
three key elements:

Food

Talk

Discussion

Guests arrive: welcome them, put them at ease, introduce them to each other. Keep the conversation fun and light and try to avoid talking about deep or heavy topics.

Food: is an important part of Alpha. Eating a simple meal together creates community and helps build friendships.

Worship music: this might feel a bit awkward on the first session so it's worth explaining that the guests don't have to join in if they don't want to.

Talk: the talks are designed to engage and inspire conversation. Generally thirty minutes long, they can be given as a live talk or played as a video. They explore the big issues around faith.

Discussion: the most important part of Alpha where guests get to say exactly what they think. It's low key, no pressure, and great fun.

Finish on time: have a set finish time and stick to it so guests know when they can leave.

Remember: no pressure, no follow up, no charge.

The perfect size for the small group is

12

Ideally two hosts, two helpers, and around eight guests.

11

Three keys to hosting a great Alpha small group

LOVE

Alpha is about sharing God's love through friendship.

"We loved you so much, we were delighted to share with you not only the gospel of God but *our lives as well"* (1 Thessalonians 2:8, emphasis added).

The greatest thing you can do as a host or helper is to share your life with your guests and to love and respect them.

"People come to church for a variety of reasons, but they stay for only one—friendship."

John Wimber,
Founder of Vineyard Church

LISTEN

Alpha is a chance for the guests to ask anything and say what they think.

The role of the hosts and helpers is to listen; not to have all the answers or to win an argument. Love them, be interested in them, and be respectful towards them.

"[People] are never so likely to settle a question rightly as when they discuss it freely."

Thomas Macaulay

The model for the Alpha small group is not teacher-pupil, but host-guest. It is vital to give guests the opportunity to respond to what they have heard and to ask questions in a safe, non-threatening environment.

Groups can be ruined by one of two things:
• Hosts and helpers speaking too much;
• Allowing one guest to dominate the discussion.

Role of the host:
• Greet newcomers to the group.
• Introduce guests to one another.
• Facilitate the discussion.
• Pray regularly for the small group.

Role of the helper:
• Look after the needs of guests.
• Handle administration for the group.
• Support the discussion with helpful comments, but do not speak too much.
• Pray quietly for each guest during the small group discussion.

Six tips for facilitating a great discussion:

1. **Ask open-ended questions.**
2. **Be encouraging.**
3. **Be yourself.**
4. **Answer the ice breaker questions, but refrain from answering other questions.**

   Exceptions to asking "What does anyone else think?"

   Questions of fact
   E.g., how many gospels are there?
   E.g., where are the toilets?

   Direct questions
   E.g., why are you a Christian?
   E.g., when did it first make sense for you?

   Difficult questions
   In the first session, make a note of everyone's questions.
   If you don't know the answer, tell guests that you'll find out and get back to them next session.

   Recommended reading
   Searching Issues by Nicky Gumbel.
   Chapters include:
   "Why Does God Allow Suffering?"
   "What About Other Religions?"
   "Is There a Conflict Between Science and Christianity?"
   "Is the Trinity Unbiblical, Unbelievable, and Irrelevant?"
   "What About the New Spirituality?"
   "Does Religion Do More Harm Than Good?"
   "Is Faith Irrational?"

5. **Don't be afraid of silence.**
6. **Rephrase the question.**

LAUGH

The experience in the Alpha small group should be low key, relaxed, and fun.

Avoid intensity.

In the first session, break the ice with a game and questions to get to know the guests:
1. Name game
2. Ask, "How and why did you end up coming to Alpha?"
3. Ask, "If it turned out there was a God after all, and you could ask one question, what would it be?"

Remember that laughter is a key component of Alpha.

Have fun and enjoy the journey.

Finally, pray for your Alpha

Prayer undergirds everything we do in Alpha, from beginning to end.

Before you begin
- The pre-session team prayer meeting is vital; a chance to pray for yourself, the team, and the guests in your group.
- Divide up the group between the hosts and helpers and commit to praying for each guest on a weekly basis.

From the front
- In general, we want to make the guests feel at ease with us, so we avoid public prayer. However, at the end of session 4—"How Can I Have Faith?", there is an opportunity for guests to join in a simple prayer asking Jesus into their life, if they want to.
- We don't say "grace" or pray before the meal.

In your small group
- The topic of prayer is introduced in session 5—"Why and How Do I Pray?"
- You may want to offer to say a short closing prayer at the end of the discussion on session 5 or in any of the subsequent sessions—"Would anyone mind if I said a short prayer to finish?"
- At some point you may feel it's appropriate to give your guests an opportunity to pray out loud:
  - go around the group and ask each person if there's anything they'd like prayer for;
  - a host should start with a very short prayer; long eloquent prayers may be impressive, but they discourage others from praying;
  - give space for those who would like to pray, to do so;

- one of the helpers should not pray, to avoid putting pressure on any guests who may not want to pray;
- a host should finish with a short, simple prayer.

It is important that the guests have experienced group prayer before the session "Does God Heal Today?", where there will be an opportunity for the guests to pray for one another.

Training 2
Prayer & the Weekend

The aim of this session is to give you all the tools you'll need to pray with and for the guests on the Alpha weekend.

The weekend is a crucial part of Alpha:
- Time to get away from the usual routines;
- Time to deepen friendships;
- Time and space to think and pray;
- An opportunity to experience the Holy Spirit.

What is prayer ministry?

- Ministry in the broadest sense means "serving" others.
- "Prayer ministry" means serving others through prayer; "meeting the needs of others on the basis of God's resources" (John Wimber).
- It is the activity of the Holy Spirit that transforms every aspect of Alpha.
- "Come Holy Spirit" *(Veni Sancte Spiritus)*—the oldest prayer of the church.
- We offer ourselves to God as His servants and leave the rest to Him.

Small Group 1 (Saturday morning):

"There are different kinds of gifts, but the same Spirit distributes them. There are different kinds of service, but the same Lord. There are different kinds of working, but in all of them and in everyone it is the same God at work. Now to each one the manifestation of the Spirit is given for the common good. To one there is given through the Spirit a message of wisdom, to another a message of knowledge by means of the same Spirit, to another faith by the same Spirit, to another gifts of healing by that one Spirit, to another miraculous powers, to another prophecy, to another distinguishing between spirits, to another speaking in different kinds of tongues, and to still another the interpretation of tongues. All these are the work of one and the same Spirit, and he distributes them to each one, just as he determines."

1 Corinthians 12:4–11

This discussion is key to facilitating the rest of the weekend:
- Read 1 Corinthians 12:4–11 verse by verse with the group; perhaps suggest that each person reads one verse.
- Ask guests what they think each of the spiritual gifts mentioned might mean.

- Make sure you cover, in particular, the gifts of prophecy and speaking in tongues, as these come up in the talk "How Can I Be Filled with the Holy Spirit?"
- Hosts and helpers should wait until the guests have shared their opinions and experiences before sharing their own.

How to pray

1. RESPECT THE INDIVIDUAL

- Sit near your group so that you can easily pray for them.
- Encourage everyone to stand during the worship music and as the music subsides, be prepared to move and pray for the guests.
- Offer to pray for each member of your group in turn: men pray with men; women pray with women.
- Ask if there is anything specific you can pray for.
- They may want to pray a prayer of commitment to Jesus:
  - you could use the prayer in the *Why Jesus?* booklet p.18;
  - you could use your own prayer: "sorry," "thank you," "please."
- They may want to receive a gift of the Spirit.
- Confidentiality is important:
  - don't pray loudly, nor gossip with others;
  - exceptions: if in doubt, seek the advice of your Alpha Leader or church pastor/priest/minister.
- Explain what will happen.

2. REMEMBER THE BIBLE

- Pray in line with the Word of God: the Spirit of God and the Bible never conflict.
- Build on the Bible's promises to encourage and strengthen:
  - freedom from guilt (Romans 8:1).
  - assurances of repentance (Psalm 51).
  - release from fear (Psalm 91).
  - God's guidance (Psalm 37:5).
  - power to overcome temptation (1 Corinthians 10:13).
  - peace in times of anxiety (Philippians 4:6–7).
  - faith in times of doubt (Matthew 7:7–11).

3. RELY ON THE HOLY SPIRIT

"In the same way, the Spirit helps us in our weakness. We do not know what we ought to pray for, but the Spirit himself intercedes for us" (Romans 8:26).

- Pray simple prayers: "Come Holy Spirit;" "Thank you that you love [guest's name]."
- Trust in Jesus' promises: expect the Holy Spirit to come (Luke 11:13).
- Don't be afraid of silence—wait and listen to God.
- If you feel God is saying something, ask yourself:
  - is it in line with the Bible?
  - is it strengthening, encouraging, comforting?
- Keep your eyes open: watch what is happening.
- Avoid intensity: no special "prayer voice," religious language, eccentricity.
- Avoid laying unnecessary burdens on guests, e.g., lack of faith.
- Avoid praying about sensitive subjects: relationships, children, jobs, money.
- Avoid criticizing other denominations or churches.

"… the one who prophesies speaks to people for their strengthening, encouraging and comfort" (1 Corinthians 14:3).

4. RELAX AND TRUST GOD

- Ask: "What do you sense is happening?" or "Do you sense God saying something?"
- Refuse to believe that nothing has happened.
- Hold on to God's promises (Matthew 7:11).
- Reassure guests that God's promises do not depend on our feelings—some may have physical manifestations, others may feel nothing but God is still at work.

Section 2
Small Group Questions

Hosts' and helpers' preparation

- Each job within the team is vitally important. If you are unable to do the job you've been given, please let the Alpha administrator know.
- Please ensure that everyone goes to the team meeting before each session— where important notices and helpful reminders are given.

Running order suggestions for a typical Alpha session

- **6.00 pm***
  Prayer and briefing meeting for all hosts and helpers: everyone needs to be clear where their group is sitting for both the meal and discussion time.

- **6.30 pm**
  When the meeting ends, hosts and helpers go to welcome their guests.

- **6.30–7.00 pm**
  As guests arrive, the Alpha administrator should allocate them to a group and introduce them to a runner who will show them to their group.

One host should stay with the group at all times and the other helpers and hosts can show guests where to pick up their meal. You may have friends who you want to chat with, but remember that your group is your number one priority. You can catch up with your friends another time!

- **7.00 pm**
  Food should be served as quickly as possible to avoid long lines and to allow small groups to talk during the mealtime. Money for the meal can be collected at the serving point (with a sign, "Suggested Donation").

- **7.28 pm**
  Encourage guests to move their chairs if necessary in order to see the worship music leader and speaker.

- **7.30 pm**
  Welcome and announcements; book recommendations; introduce speaker; hand over to worship leader.

- **7.45 pm**
  Talk starts.

- **8.15 pm**
  Talk ends. Swiftly get into your small group for the discussion time. Delegate the coffee serving to one of the helpers.

- **9.15 pm**
  Make sure you finish on time after each session. As the discussion draws to a close, suggest going on to somewhere (e.g., café) for a drink together and/or help guests who may be interested in buying books and resources.

You may want to think about how people can purchase books from the recommended reading list, either by directing them online or selling books through your own bookstore.

*Running times have been given as a guide only

Recommended reading

Session 1 – Is There More to Life Than This?
What's So Amazing About Grace? Philip Yancey

Session 2 – Who Is Jesus?
Mere Christianity, C. S. Lewis
Jesus Is, Judah Smith

Session 3 – Why Did Jesus Die?
The Cross of Christ, John Stott
Searching Issues, Nicky Gumbel
Mud, Sweat and Tears, Bear Grylls

Session 4 – How Can I Have Faith?
The Reason for God, Tim Keller
Life Change, Mark Elsdon-Dew

Session 5 – Why and How Do I Pray?
Too Busy Not To Pray, Bill Hybels
God on Mute, Pete Greig

Session 6 – Why and How Should I Read the Bible?
Why Trust the Bible? Amy Orr-Ewing
30 days, Nicky Gumbel
bibleinoneyear.org, Nicky and Pippa Gumbel
Bible in One Year app for iPhone/Android

Session 7 – How Does God Guide Us?
Chasing the Dragon, Jackie Pullinger

Sessions 8-11 – Recommended reading provided during the weekend

Session 12 – How Can I Resist Evil?
Screwtape Letters, C. S. Lewis
Cafe Theology, Mike Lloyd

Session 13 – Why and How Should I Tell Others?
Searching Issues, Nicky Gumbel
Lord... Help My Unbelief, John Young

Session 14 – Does God Heal Today?
Power Evangelism, John Wimber

Session 15 – What About the Church?
Questions of Life, Nicky Gumbel

Is There More to Life Than This?

Admin

1. Ensure that you have registered everyone in the group and that each person has a name badge.
2. Serve drinks and snacks before beginning the discussion.
3. Introduce yourself and welcome everyone to the group.
4. Explain the format for each session and the number of sessions.
5. Highlight: no pressure, no follow up, no charge.
6. Explain the format and purpose of the small group discussion.
7. Reassure the guests that you always finish on time.

Icebreakers

These games will enable the group to remember each other's names and get to know one another.

Name Game

- "Everyone think of a positive adjective that starts with the same letter as your first name" e.g., "Jovial John" or "Happy Helen" OR "Everyone think of a famous person with the same first name as you" e.g., "Justin Bieber," "Sandra Bullock."

- Start with the person on your left. They must say their name and positive adjective or celebrity name. The next person must say their name and adjective or celebrity name and that of the person before them.

- Each person must try and repeat all the names of the guests preceding them from memory. The host is the last person to go and repeats the names of everyone in the group.

- Be quick to help any guests who might find this more difficult.

Desert Island Game (if you have time)

- "If you were stuck on a desert island and you could take one thing (not a person) with you, and you already have the Bible and the complete works of Shakespeare, what would you take?"

- OR "Which person from history would you like to be stuck in an elevator with, and why?"

"How and why did you end up coming here today?"

- This gives the rest of the group permission to say what they really think. Try to draw more out of guests if they are a bit hesitant. Start with the guest you think is most reluctant/hostile about doing Alpha to encourage other guests to open up and be honest.

"If it turned out there was a God after all, and you could ask one question, what would it be?"

- Encourage guests, "These are great questions."
- Write the questions down on a piece of paper with a view to coming back to them at the end of Alpha.

Finish on time and carry on discussion elsewhere (e.g., café) for those who want to.

Who Is Jesus?

Admin

Welcome the group, then go around and ask each person to introduce themselves briefly. Welcome any new guests and ask them, "How and why did you end up coming here today?" Update the registration list. Add any new names and contact details and correct any mistakes from the previous session.

Key Concept

Understanding the evidence regarding the historical claims of Jesus Christ.

Guests come to Alpha with a variety of ideas about Jesus. Many of their views would fall into the "folklore/legend" category. Others would see Jesus as a wonderful man, great moral teacher, or religious leader. There are some who really have no idea about Jesus. The goal this week is to get their ideas on the table and begin to help them sort out the evidence that either questions or confirms their assumptions. Discussions around Jesus that may surface include: Was Jesus a real, historical person? Was He more than a wonderful man? Was He more than a great moral teacher or religious leader?

Questions for discussion

1. What did you think or feel about the talk?

2. What makes you happy?

3. What do you think about Jesus?

4. If you had a chance to meet Jesus, how would you feel and what would you say to Him?

Additional questions (if needed):

5. Before you heard the talk tonight, what was your concept of Jesus? Has it changed? If so, in what way?

6. What aspects of the evidence presented tonight did you find convincing/not convincing?

Why Did Jesus Die?

Admin

Introduce any new guests. Pass around the registration list. Add any new names and contact details and correct any mistakes from the previous session.

Key Concept

If we are honest, we all have to admit that we do things we know are wrong.

This week we are looking at the problem of sin, God's solution, and the result of Jesus' death. We may have heard that Jesus died on the cross, but we are left asking the question, "Why did He die?" Does Jesus' death really have relevance to our lives today? Why are we so good at rationalizing our mistakes and feeling superior to others?

Really listen for what the guests have to say around this pivotal week of Alpha.

Questions for discussion

This is often the session when the subject of "suffering" arises (see *Searching Issues* chapter "Why Does God Allow Suffering?").

1. What did you think or feel about the talk?

2. What does the word "forgiveness" mean to you?

3. Have you ever had to forgive anyone? How did you do it?

4. What does the word "sin" mean to you?

Additional question (if needed):

5. What is your reaction to Jesus' death?

How Can I Have Faith?

Admin

Introduce any new guests. Update the registration list and amend if needed. This is a good session to mention the Alpha weekend for the first time. Give the dates to the guests.

Key Concept

This week we are looking at the evidence for believing in Christianity. The message takes the perspective of a person who has decided to believe the claims of Christianity. How can that person make sure they have made the right decision? Many will still be exploring faith so continue to let them ask questions and let the group respond. Encourage them to consider what obstacles might keep them from having faith.

Questions for discussion

You may find that guests have questions, for example, about other religions (see *Searching Issues* chapter "What About Other Religions?").

1. What did you think or feel about the talk?

2. What does faith mean to you?

3. What do you think about the evidence for Christianity that was presented here?

4. How can a person have faith in someone that he/she can't see?

Why and How Do I Pray?

Admin

This is a good session to encourage guests to attend the Alpha weekend. Mention the cost and the possibility of scholarships.

Key Concept

Prayer is at the heart of Christianity: because at the heart of Christianity is a relationship with God.

Surveys indicate that most people pray. Even people who don't consider themselves religious find themselves praying from time to time. Where do we take our fears and anxieties? Sometimes our worries seem like they are going to crush us. Other times we experience a calm we can't explain, but it doesn't last. Is there something/someone bigger we can trust? Still these questions may remain: If God knows our needs, why should we pray about them? What is the value of prayer? Take time to introduce prayer this week at the end of the small group time.

Questions for discussion

1. What did you think or feel about the talk?

2. Have you ever tried praying? How did it go?

3. What do you think about the idea of God answering prayer?

4. Have you ever prayed and a coincidence happened?

Additional question (if needed):

5. In the talk, various reasons for praying are given.
    Which of these do you relate to and why?

Why and How Should I Read the Bible?

Admin

Remind the group about the Alpha weekend. Ask someone who has benefited from a previous one to describe their experience. Begin to gather names and collect payment if needed.

Key Concept

The Bible is one way God can speak to us.

This week we will look at how to read the Bible. Encourage the guests to get a Bible in a version that they can understand. Remember that when a guest hears God for themselves in the Bible, they will remember it more than if we talk about how we hear God.

Questions for discussion

1. What did you think or feel about the talk?

2. Has anyone ever tried reading any of the Bible? How was your experience?

3. How do you feel about the idea of God speaking through the Bible?

4. Does anyone have any practical suggestions about how to read the Bible? (At an appropriate point in discussion, you might recommend the Bible in One Year app: bibleinoneyear.org.)

Additional question (if needed):

4. Have you read anything in the Bible that has challenged an aspect of your beliefs or behavior?

....

....

....

....

....

....

....

....

....

....

....

....

....

....

....

....

....

....

....

....

....

....

How Does God Guide Us?

Admin

Arrange transportation for the Alpha weekend if necessary.

Key Concept

Tonight we want to discuss the idea that God has a plan for our lives.

Be attentive to the creative ways He has revealed His plan to your guests. Try to create ways for people who feel like they have "messed up" in life to see that God is the God of the second, third, fourth chance.

Questions for discussion

1. What did you think or feel about the talk?

2. Over the last few weeks, has anyone had a sense that God might be guiding them?

3. How do you feel about the idea of God having a plan for your life?

4. What are the ways that God may speak to people today? Have you ever experienced this?

5. What should we do if we believe we have made a mess of our lives?

Additional Question: (This could be a good addition to question 2: What is a risk you could take to make yourself a better person or make the world a better place?) Encourage guests that many times God may be speaking to them through these desires.

Who Is the Holy Spirit?

There is no small group discussion following this session.

Encourage guests that this is a longer session and that the discussion time will follow the talk on "What does the Holy Spirit Do?" Focus on relationships and enjoy spending time with each other. For many, a day away or weekend away could be an intimidating experience. So, relax and enjoy yourself. Have fun!

What Does the Holy Spirit Do?

Questions for discussion

Read 1 Corinthians 12:4–11.

1. What do you think each of the spiritual gifts refers to? (vv. 8–10)

2. What is the gift of tongues? Does anyone have any experience with this?

3. How do you feel about the idea of God giving us supernatural gifts?

4. Does everybody have the same gifts? (vv. 4–6)
    • different gifts, works and service, but the same God

5. Why does God give spiritual gifts to people? (v. 7)
    • for the common good
    • not for our own glory

6. Mention that there will be an opportunity to hear more on this subject in the next session.

Key Concept

The Holy Spirit does a variety of things including giving new life, a newfound sense of family and unity, and new power to follow Christ. The Holy Spirit not only transforms our character, but gives us the ability to be a blessing to others as well.

Take time to discuss some of the spiritual gifts that will be mentioned in the next talk. Many people may have never had a chance to talk about these things, so encourage them to keep an open mind and focus on how these gifts could be a blessing to others.

How Can I Be Filled with the Holy Spirit?

This session is followed by a time of prayer ministry in a group setting. Spend time praying with any guests who would like prayer to be filled with the Holy Spirit (see Training 2).

Encourage guests who have further questions that you would be more than happy to discuss the teaching following the prayer time. The beauty of having a day away or weekend away is that you will have plenty of time to process the teaching and have lots of discussion. Make sure to keep the discussion alive so that guests can take their next steps.

How Can I Make the Most of the Rest of My Life?

Ask each member of the group, starting with the person who will be most open, to describe their experience of the weekend. This will give permission for any others who want to, to share their experiences. If appropriate you may wish to offer an opportunity for the group to pray for one another.

How Can I Resist Evil?

Admin

Start the small group time by asking guests to share their experiences of the Alpha weekend. (Start with the person who will be most open/positive.) This gives the guests the opportunity to express what happened to them. It can be a great encouragement to the group. Remember to include those who did not go on the weekend in the discussion by asking them what they think about what they have heard.

Key Concept

Look at the daily newspaper and we see evil all around us.

The talk about evil is intended to come the week after the Alpha Weekend, to provide guests a firm foundation of spiritual confidence. Please be sure to encourage and strengthen your group. Pray for each other to close the evening.

Questions for discussion

1. Feedback from the weekend (see notes above).

2. What did you think or feel about the talk?

3. Why do you think bad things happen?

4. Where does temptation come from?

5. How do you resist temptation?

Why and How Should I Tell Others?

Admin

If you are holding an Alpha celebration evening to mark the end of the course, this is a good time to remind guests of the date and times. Invitations can be handed out too. If possible, aim to pray together as a group at the end of this session or if you focus on inviting guests to the first session of the next Alpha, this is a good time to remind guests of the date and times.

Key Concept

It can be difficult to talk to others about the deeper or personal matters of our lives.

Certainly our faith in Christ falls into this category. Some people feel that one's faith is a private matter and should not be discussed with others. However, telling others about our faith is a natural part of our relationship with God. After this session, guests will be more prepared to invite others to the Celebration Dinner.

Questions for discussion

1. What did you think or feel about the talk?

2. Have you told any of your friends/family/colleagues at work that you are attending Alpha? What was their reaction?

3. If you did not know anything about Christianity, how would you like to be told about it?

4. What do you think/feel about the idea of telling others about your faith?

Does God Heal Today?

Admin

Remind guests about the Alpha celebration if you are planning one. Try to work out approximately how many people will be coming, including small group members and any guests they plan to invite.

This is a great week to have your leadership team gather early and spend some time in prayer, listening for specific promptings or words of knowledge that God may want you to pray for later in the evening. This session will present an opportunity for guests to receive prayer for healing. The healing may be emotional, physical, or spiritual. If you do sense that God is revealing some specific things to pray for, you may present these to the broader group before the discussion time and ask if any of the group senses that the "word of knowledge" was for them. If this is the case, encourage them to receive prayer when they are ready.

Key Concept

God is still healing today.

The Greek word that means "I save" also means "I heal." God is concerned not just about our spiritual salvation, but our whole being. One day we shall have a new and perfect body. In this life we will never reach perfection. When God heals someone miraculously today, we get a glimpse of the future when the final redemption of our bodies will take place (Romans 8:23).

Prayer for healing

- Ask your guests if there is a specific problem or illness for which they would like prayer for healing. At the same time ask if anyone would like prayer for any other issue. This is a good time to clear up any general issues about the subject of healing, so allow time for the group to discuss briefly before praying together.

- Pray for guests according to the prayer ministry guidelines (Training 2). If there are lots of guests, divide into one group of men and one group of women.

- "At one point, we never used to pray for anyone to be healed and nobody got healed. Then, we started praying for everyone to be healed, and now, *sometimes* people get healed. That's a much better percentage."

- Be prepared for someone who may want to give their life to Christ. Equally affirm those who do want to be prayed for and those who do not.

- Also be mindful to encourage guests that healing comes in many ways and is not always immediate. When we pray we pray in faith, but we trust God to do what He wills, whenever and however He chooses.

What About the Church?

Admin

Remind the group about the Alpha celebration or provide details about church on Sunday. Make a date for a small group reunion. This could possibly be at the host's home, ideally about two weeks before the next Alpha starts, or sooner if appropriate.

Ask the guests to complete the Alpha questionnaire to give feedback on their experience.

Key Concept

Today the church, as an institution, gets a lot of negative press.

Some see the church as an organization that abuses people or has some political agenda. This is certainly a different picture than what Jesus drew for His disciples when He described a church that would "prevail against the gates of hell and become hope for the world." In this session, we help people rethink their understanding of the church as an organization and begin to understand the value of Christian fellowship and to see how involvement could have a positive impact in their lives.

Questions for discussion

1. Go around the group asking each person to summarize what they have learned and experienced over the past eleven sessions. (Try to start with the most open/ positive person).

2. Ask the group what they would like to do after Alpha.
   Try to encourage them to stay connected as a group.

3. Ask each of them if there is anything they would like prayer for.

4. Pray—it's a good idea to finish the final session with prayer.

Optional questions for further discussion

1. What comes to mind when you hear the words "church" or "Christian"?

2. Look back on the last eleven sessions. Has your view changed?

3. Looking forward, in what way (if any) do you plan to continue what you've started in Alpha?

Alpha Basics

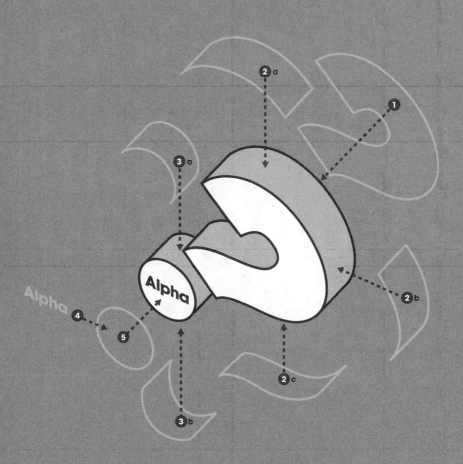

Now that you have come to the end of Alpha, what's next? Help in Alpha again or run one in your home, a café, or somewhere else in your community? Here is everything you need to know to get started.

TODAY, MORE THAN

29,000,000

PEOPLE HAVE ATTENDED ALPHA IN
MORE THAN 169 COUNTRIES.

WELCOME TO ALPHA

This guide will give you an introduction to Alpha and help you through the steps you need to run it for the first time.

WHAT IS ALPHA?

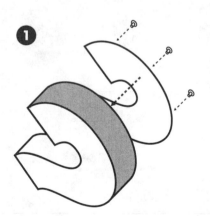

1

Alpha is a series of fifteen interactive sessions, typically run over eleven weeks, including a weekend away, where anyone can explore life and the Christian faith in a friendly, open, and informal environment.

Everyone is welcome, but Alpha is designed particularly for people who would not describe themselves as Christians or church-goers.

There's no charge to attend Alpha—it's free.

WHAT'S THE STORY?

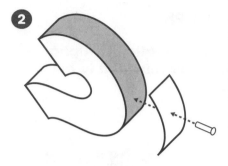

Alpha started over thirty years ago at Holy Trinity Brompton (HTB), an Anglican church in Central London, UK.

It was originally developed as a short course for people in the church. In 1990, Nicky Gumbel took over running Alpha and found that many people outside of the church were warming up to the idea of Alpha. Today, more than 29 million people have attended Alpha in more than 169 countries, and it has been translated into 112 different languages. It runs in every part of the worldwide church—the Catholic Church, the Orthodox Church, the Pentecostal Church, and all the mainline Protestant denominations.

ALPHA IS...

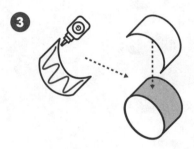

③

Alpha is based on a pattern you find in the New Testament of people bringing their friends, family, and work colleagues to meet Jesus.

Andrew brought his brother Peter; Philip brought Nathaniel; Matthew had a party and invited all his work colleagues—he said, "Come and meet Jesus!" Alpha is an easy way of saying to friends, "Come and see, come and explore your questions, come and hear about Jesus, come and see for yourself."

In Alpha we try to be:

REAL—Alpha presents the reality of who Jesus is. Those that run Alpha are real and authentic and this allows the guests to be real themselves. People are welcome to ask questions and look for answers, with no pressure to contribute and no follow up if they don't come back.

RELATIONAL—Alpha is based on genuine friendships that are built up over a few weeks and often last for years afterwards.

RELIANT—In Alpha we are reliant on the Holy Spirit because we realize that it is only God who changes people's lives; we just introduce Him.

No one can force anyone to believe anything. What we've found over the years is that if we allow people to be themselves and ask their questions, focus on building relationships and rely on the Holy Spirit, lives are changed.

ALPHA IS RUNNING IN CHURCHES, BARS, COFFEE SHOPS AND HOMES WORLDWIDE.

HOW DOES ALPHA WORK?

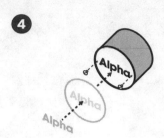

④

Every Alpha session has three key elements: a meal, a talk, and a discussion.

Food

Almost every social event is centered around food and drink. The food in Alpha allows people from different backgrounds, with a whole variety of questions and ideas about life, to come together, share a meal, and get to know one another on a deeper level.

It is best not to charge for food at Alpha— we believe that hearing about Jesus should be free. While lots of Alphas do ask for a suggested donation to help cover the costs, it doesn't have to be expensive to prepare some refreshments for our guests. Some churches ask their home groups to take turns to cook for Alpha. Each group covers the cost of the week they cook, which spreads the cost across the church, not just on one team or group. Some churches also run their Alpha in a café and just provide a nice coffee for the guests.

Talks

After some food and time to get to know one another, a short talk is given.

The fifteen talks in order (including the Alpha weekend) are:

SESSION 1
Is There More to Life Than This?

SESSION 2
Who Is Jesus?

SESSION 3
Why Did Jesus Die?

SESSION 4
How Can I Have Faith?

SESSION 5
Why and How Should I Pray?

SESSION 6
Why and How Should I Read the Bible?

SESSION 7
How Does God Guide Us?

—

WEEKEND SESSION 1
Who Is the Holy Spirit?

WEEKEND SESSION 2
What Does the Holy Spirit Do?

WEEKEND SESSION 3
How Can I Be Filled with the Holy Spirit?

WEEKEND SESSION 4
How Can I Make the Most of the Rest of My Life?

SESSION 8
How Can I Resist Evil?

SESSION 9
Why and How Should I Tell Others?

SESSION 10
Does God Heal Today?

SESSION 11
What About the Church?

Sometimes it isn't possible to spread Alpha across eleven weeks, so we've made some resources available (downloadable from Alpha Builder at **alphausa.org/run** and **run.alphacanada.org**), which combine a couple of the talks. However, if you can, try to run Alpha for the full eleven weeks. The more time you have with the guests, the greater opportunity you have to make real friendships and to allow a real process of discovery to happen. No one has to commit upfront to all eleven sessions but by the end we find that they are wishing that there were far more than eleven.

There are two options for delivering the talks: you can give the talks yourself or there are a variety of video resources available to watch. What you decide to do will depend on your audience and your venue. It might be strange to stand up and deliver a talk if your Alpha is held in your college dorm with three of your friends and a box of pizza, and it might not be possible to watch a video if your Alpha is held on the beach with your surfer buddies. That's why we've created a few different resources so that, whatever your Alpha looks like, there is something to fit your context.

The scripts and all of the video resources are available for free online from Alpha Builder at alphausa.org/run and run.alphacanada.org

Discussion
The heart of Alpha is the small group. This is where people can ask questions, talk through issues, build relationships, and experience what the Christian life really looks like.

There are a few really practical things that are worth remembering, which can make the difference between an awkward conversation and a real sense of friendship and family in your groups.

The thing that can most affect the success or failure of a small group is choosing and training your hosts and helpers. Alpha small groups are not like other small groups. The host's focus is on allowing guests the space to ask questions rather than offering all the answers. Even though the leaders you have picked may have lots of experience leading groups and may have hosted Alpha groups before, it's still essential to train all the hosts and helpers.

All the training for how to run an Alpha small group is available online on Alpha Builder at **alphausa.org/run** and **run.alphacanada.org**.

HOW DO WE GET STARTED?

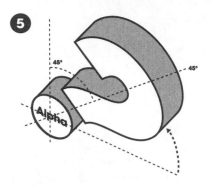

⑤

45°

45°

Alpha

When should we run Alpha?

There are a few helpful things to think through when deciding the dates and times to run your Alpha.

Dates

The first thing to do is to plan your dates. Try to avoid booking your Alpha over any holidays or events to avoid long gaps between sessions or guests being unable to attend. For example, running Alpha over Christmas or during school breaks might mean some of your guests will not be able to attend during those weeks.

You also need to think about two dates for training your team and a date for a launch party, if you are having one.

Timings

A typical Alpha runs in the evening but Alpha can be held at any time of day, you just need to work out the best time for the people you are trying to invite. For example, if you are running Alpha with college students, an early morning breakfast might not be the best option. Whatever time you choose, make sure that you have enough time for food, a talk, and a discussion.

The following is an example schedule for morning or evening.

Evening:

7:00 – Food
7:30 – Welcome
7:35 – Worship Music
7:45 – Talk
8:15 – Discussion Groups
9:15 – End

Morning:

09:45 – Breakfast and Coffee
10:15 – Welcome
10:20 – Worship Music
10:30 – Talk
11:00 – Discussion Group
12:00 – End

Where should we run Alpha?

Alpha is currently run in homes, cafés, churches, pubs, and all sorts of other locations all around the world. It doesn't matter what venue you choose, just try to make the space welcoming and conducive to good conversation.

How should we invite people?

Each year Alpha produces a range of invitational materials, which can be found online. There are posters, postcards, banners, and other print materials, as well as a range of images and videos to use online.

These invitational materials are a great way of letting your wider community know about Alpha, but the main way people come is still through being invited by a friend. Make sure that your church or organization gets on board and that everyone invites their friends along.

Some churches host an informal "Launch Party" to make it even easier to invite guests along to hear about Alpha and what it involves.

Who should be on the team?

Choosing the right team is really important. The people that host and help in the small groups need to be the best people to both welcome new people into the community and guide discussions in a way that allows for real exploration.

The most helpful question to ask is, "Would I be comfortable with putting my best non-Christian friend in the group with these hosts?" If the answer is no, then it is important to keep looking for the right people.

It is also really important to train your team well. Although Alpha has a simple format, there are a few crucial things to remember when running a small group. Even if your hosts and helpers have done Alpha several times, it's still a great idea to do the training before you start.

All the materials you need to train your team are available on Alpha Builder at **alphausa.org/run** and **run.alphacanada.org**.

Plan your Alpha weekend away

A crucial part of Alpha is the weekend or day away. This can feel like a difficult thing to organize but it doesn't have to be.

It is a really important part of Alpha and is often the part which guests find most transformative, so it's worth putting effort into running one if you can. A good way to make the process easier is to pair up with another Alpha in your city and run a weekend together.

For top tips and more information on exactly what is involved, there is more training available about the Alpha weekend on Alpha Builder.

Promote your Alpha

Now that you've used Alpha Builder to organize your Alpha, make sure that you promote it so that people can find you on the website. Often we hear of people who attend Alpha just from searching for it in their area or on our website. It's great if they can find your Alpha and come along.

For Alpha Builder, go to alphausa.org/run or run.alphacanada.org.

Pray

It is really important to pray for your Alpha. Here are a few suggestions:

1. Get your whole church praying

Spend some time praying for Alpha in your services, small groups, and prayer meetings. Even if your Alpha will take place on your college campus, in your local coffee shop, or somewhere else outside of the church, get everyone you can praying. Not only does this make a difference, but it also helps keep Alpha in the minds of the church and reminds them to invite their friends to the next one.

2. Get people to pray together before each session of Alpha

During the administration meeting at the start of each Alpha session, take time to pray with the Alpha hosts, helpers, and team—pray for one another, the talk, and the guests.

3. Get hosts and helpers praying for each guest

Encourage hosts and helpers to pray for every guest in their group every day by name throughout Alpha.

4. Get the guests praying when they are ready

It's exciting when members of your group pray aloud for the first time, begin offering to pray for one another, or report on answered prayers from the week before. When the group is ready, normally on the week when we talk about prayer, we model a nice simple prayer and give others the chance to pray if they want to. Some of those first simple prayers are the best.

CONNECT WITH ALPHA

Let's connect
We welcome any opportunity to speak with you. Whether it's hearing your vision, or simply assisting you with a question, our team is waiting to talk with you.

alphausa.org/contact
800.362.5742

alphacanada.org/connect
800.743.0899

carribean.alpha.org/contact
868.671.0133

Go deeper in the Word
Start your day with the Bible in One Year, a free Bible reading app with commentary by Nicky and Pippa Gumbel. Receive a daily email or audio commentary coordinated with the Bible in One Year reading plan.

alpha.org/bioy

Connect with us on Social Media

@AlphaUSA | @AlphaCanada | @AlphaLatAm

Join the conversation: #TryAlpha #RunAlpha

ALPHA RESOURCES

Why Jesus?

This booklet may be given to all participants at the start of Alpha. "The clearest, best illustrated and most challenging short presentation of Jesus that I know." – Michael Green

Why Christmas?
Why Easter?

The Christmas and Easter versions of *Why Jesus?*

Questions of Life

Alpha in book form. In fifteen compelling chapters, Nicky Gumbel points the way to an authentic Christianity which is exciting and relevant to the world today.

Searching Issues

The seven issues most often raised by participants on Alpha: suffering, other religions, does religion do more harm than good, is faith irrational, new spirituality, science and Christianity, and the Trinity.

The Jesus Lifestyle

Studies in the Sermon on the Mount showing how Jesus' teaching flies in the face of modern lifestyle and presents us with a radical alternative.

30 Days

Nicky Gumbel selects thirty passages from the Old and New Testament which can be read over thirty days. It is designed for those in Alpha and others who are interested in beginning to explore the Bible.

All titles are by Nicky Gumbel, pioneer of Alpha

Alpha USA
1635 Emerson Lane
Naperville, IL 60540

800.362.5742

questions@alphausa.org
alphausa.org

@alphausa

Alpha Canada
#101-26 Fourth Street
New Westminister, BC V3L 5M4

800.743.0899

office@alphacanada.org
alphacanada.org

@alphacanada

Alpha in the Caribbean
Holy Trinity Brompton
Brompton Road
London SW7 1JA UK

+44 (0) 845.644.7544

americas@alpha.org
caribbean.alpha.org

@alphacaribbean

Pay It Forward

Alpha exists to serve churches in their mission to help people discover and develop a relationship with Jesus, and we provide all of our resources available at no cost to churches and guests. In fact, Alpha is 100% funded by donations large and small. Millions of people around the world have met Jesus through Alpha because of the generosity of friends like you.

If you would like to help make this possible for more churches and guests to experience, we would be so grateful. You can give online at:

USA: alphausa.org/give | Canada: donate.alphacanada.org